Bible Quotes of Love and Wisdom

WITH ANNOTATIONS BY GARY STEELE

Bible Quotes of Love and Wisdom

WITH ANNOTATIONS BY GARY STEELE

AND I WAS DAILY HIS DELIGHT,
REJOICING BEFORE HIM ALWAYS,
REJOICING IN HIS INHABITED WORLD AND
DELIGHTING IN THE HUMAN RACE.

'AND NOW, MY CHILDREN, LISTEN TO ME:
HAPPY ARE THOSE WHO KEEP MY WAYS.
HEAR INSTRUCTION AND BE WISE, AND
DO NOT NEGLECT IT.

HAPPY IS THE ONE WHO LISTENS TO ME,
WATCHING DAILY AT MY GATES, WAITING
BESIDE MY DOORS. FOR WHOEVER FINDS
ME FINDS LIFE AND OBTAINS FAVOR
FROM THE LORD;

BUT THOSE WHO MISS ME INJURE
THEMSELVES; ALL WHO HATE ME LOVE
DEATH.' (WHEN WE ARE CENTERED,
POISED AND EQUILIBRATED.)

FOREWORD

I am not arrogant enough to think that I am some sort of expert on the Bible. Or that I can interrupt the Bible for other people. That is not the intent of this booklet. The intent behind writing this was to pull out for me what was relevant to my understanding of love and wisdom. I searched through the Bible finding every passage that contained the words love and wisdom. I then pulled out the ones that where relevant to my beliefs about life, God, equilibrium and love. I believe everyone who reads the Bible finds their own meaning in what they read. If you happen to find what I found inspiring, inspiring to you then enjoy it and use it in your own journey toward love.

I hope you find the journey of discovery as inspiring as I do.

Love, Light and Wisdom,

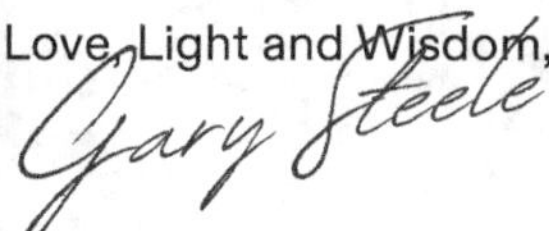

> **Wisdom and knowledge are granted to you. I will also give you riches, possessions, and honor, such as none of the kings had who were before you ever had**

— 2 Chronicles 1.12

The greatest riches come after we love the outer to a state of silence and we then see the magnificence of our own being.

For everything there is a season,
And a time for every matter under heaven:
A time to be born, and a time to die;
A time to plant, and a time to pluck up what
is planted;
A time to kill, and a time to heal;
A time to break down, and a time
to build up;
A time to weep, and a time to laugh; A time
to mourn, and a time to dance; A time to
throw away stones, and a time to gather
stones together;
A time to embrace, And a time to refrain
from embracing;
A time to seek, and a time to lose;
A time to keep, and a time to throw away;
A time to tear, and a time to sew;
A time to keep silence, and a time to speak;
A time to love, and a time to hate,
A time for war, and a time for peace.

— Ecclesiastes 3:1-8

The will of God is Equilibrium.

THEIR TENT-CORD IS PLUCKED UP WITHIN THEM AND THEY DIE DEVOID OF WISDOM.

— Job 4.21

Love and Gratitude for our life as it is for what it is gives us life. The opposite takes life away.

With God are wisdom and strength; he has counsel and understanding.

— Job 12.13

When we see equilibrium we see God.

WITH HIM ARE STRENGTH AND WISDOM;

THE DECEIVED AND THE DECEIVER ARE HIS.

— Job 12.16

In the inner is wisdom the outer is the deceiver.

If you would only keep silent, that would be your wisdom.

— Job 13.5

In the inner silence of equanimity is where wisdom resides.

HAVE YOU LISTENED IN THE COUNCIL OF GOD AND DO YOU LIMIT WISDOM TO YOURSELF?

— Job 15.8

When we are centered, poised and equilibrated.

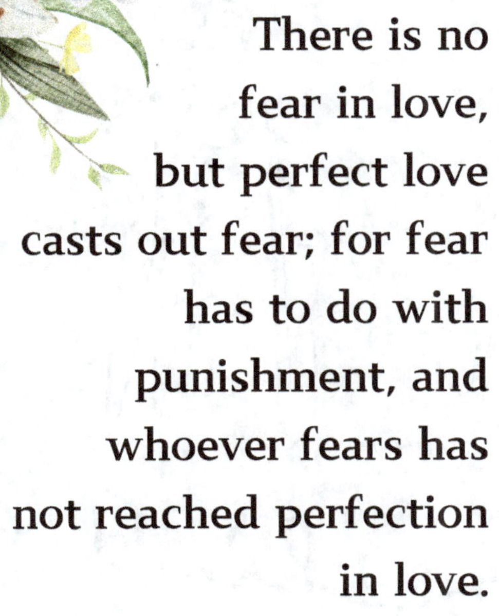

There is no
fear in love,
but perfect love
casts out fear; for fear
has to do with
punishment, and
whoever fears has
not reached perfection
in love.

— 1 John 4.18

Get to the center and only love exists.

Jesus

When we are centered, poised and equilibrated.

Those who say, 'I love God', and hate their brothers or sisters, are liars; for those who do not love a brother or sister* whom they have seen, cannot love God whom they have not seen.

— 1 John 4.20

The commandment we
have from him is this:
those who love God must love
their brothers and sisters
also.

— I John 4.21

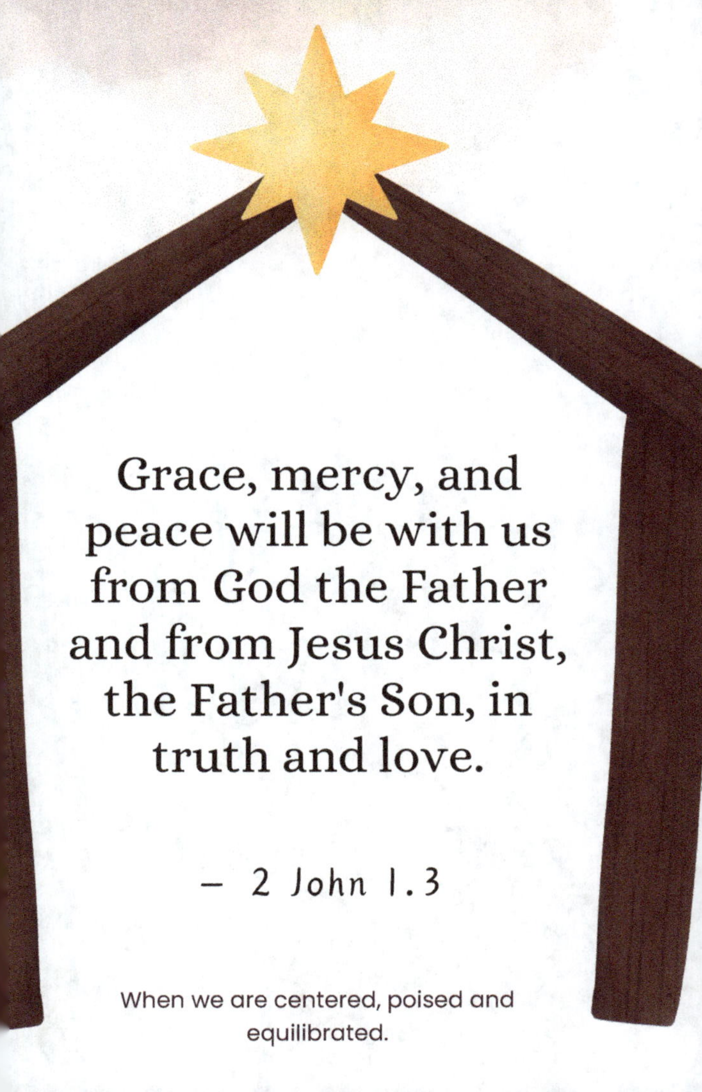

Grace, mercy, and peace will be with us from God the Father and from Jesus Christ, the Father's Son, in truth and love.

— 2 John 1.3

When we are centered, poised and equilibrated.

But the aim of such
instruction is
love that comes
from a pure
heart, and a
good conscience
and a sincere faith.

— 1 Timothy 1.5

For the love of money is a root of all kinds of evil, and in their eagerness to be rich some have wandered away from the faith and pierced themselves with many pains.

— 1 Timothy 6.10

All things have pains and pleasures and the yare perfectly balanced 50/50

KEEP YOUR LIVES FREE FROM THE LOVE OF MONEY, AND BE CONTENT WITH WHAT YOU HAVE; FOR HE HAS SAID,

'I will never leave you or forsake you.'

— HEBREWS 13.5

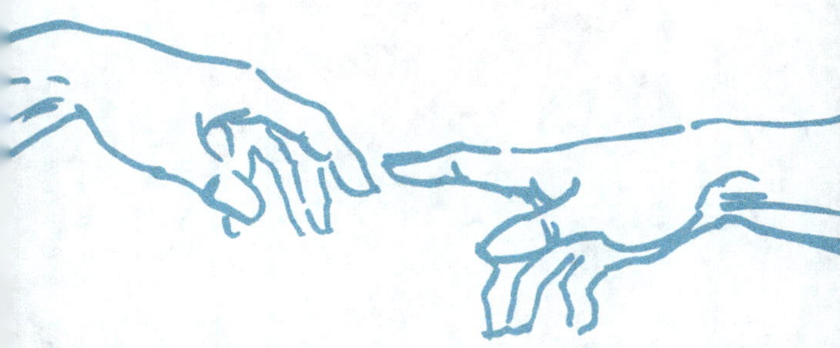

Build wealth through your inspirations, don't chase money for the sake of chasing money, it will feel empty when you catch it.

You do well if you really fulfill the royal law according to the scripture, `You shall love your neighbor as yourself.'

— James 2.8

NOW THAT YOU HAVE PURIFIED YOUR SOULS BY YOUR OBEDIENCE TO THE TRUTH SO THAT YOU HAVE GENUINE MUTUAL LOVE, LOVE ONE ANOTHER DEEPLY FROM THE HEART.

— 1 PETER 1.22

Open your heart, open your life.

But do not ignore this one fact, beloved, that with the Lord one day is like a thousand years, and a thousand years are like one day.

— 2 PETER 3.8

Presence

Whoever loves a brother or sister
lives in the light.

— 2 PETER 3.8

Open your heart to love.

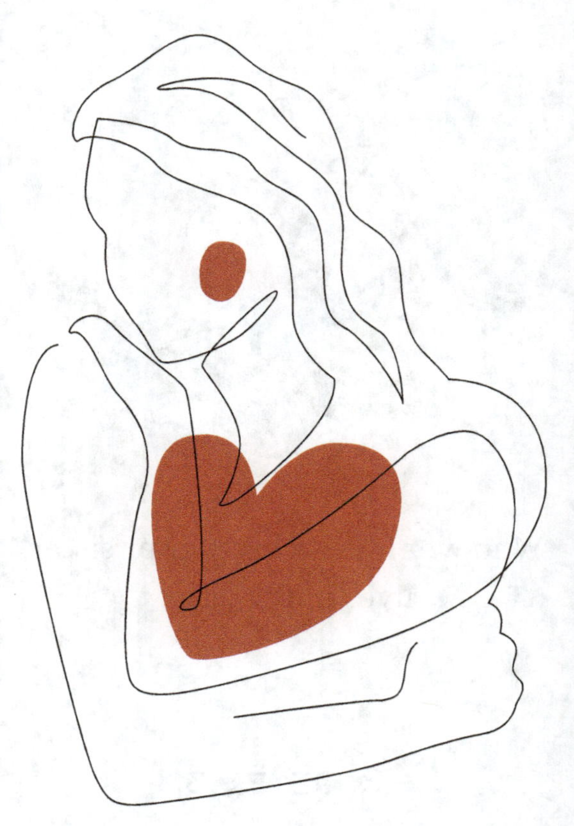

No one has ever seen God; if we love one another, God lives in us, and his love is perfected in us.

— I John 4.12

Wisdom of life.

So we have known and believe the love that God has for us. God is love, and those who abide in love abide in God, and God abides in them.

— 1 John 4.16

Listen to your inner voice, the voice of your soul and the wisdom of the universe is yours.

BUT WHERE SHALL WISDOM BE FOUND? AND WHERE IS THE PLACE OF UNDERSTANDING?

– Job 28.12

See the balance, have wisdom.

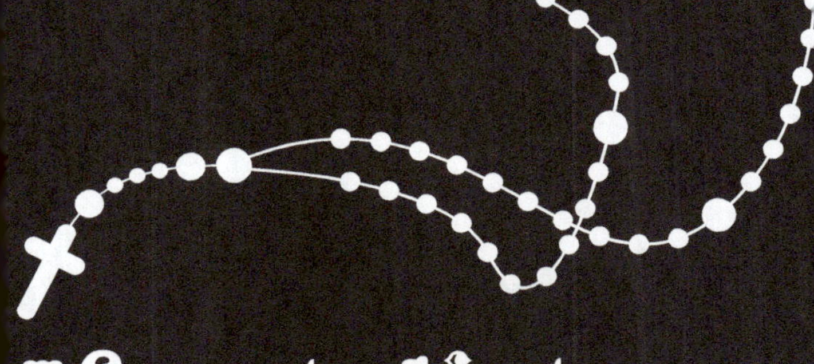

If not, listen to me; be silent, and I will teach you wisdom.

— JOB 33.33

The inner voice, it is your souls breath speaking
to you all that is yours to do.

I believe

20 Wisdom cries out in the street; in the squares she raises her voice.21 At the busiest corner she cries out; at the entrance of the city gates she speaks:

22 How long, O simple ones, will you love being simple? How long will scoffers delight in their scoffing and fools hate knowledge?

23 Give heed to my reproof; I will pour out my thoughts to you; I will make my words known to you.

24 Because I have called and you refused, have stretched out my hand and no one heeded,

25 and because you have ignored all my counsel and would have none of my reproof

— Proverbs 1.15-25

Listen to the inner voice, it is waiting.

My child, if you accept my words and
treasure up my commandments within
you,
2 making your ear attentive to wisdom
and inclining your heart to understanding;
3 if you indeed cry out for insight,
and raise your voice for
understanding;
4 if you seek it like silver,
and search for it as for hidden
treasures-
5 then you will understand the
fear of the Lord and find the
knowledge of God.
6 For the Lord gives wisdom;
from his mouth come knowledge and
understanding;

— PROVERBS 2.6

FOR WISDOM WILL COME INTO YOUR HEART, AND KNOWLEDGE WILL BE PLEASANT TO YOUR SOUL;

— Proverbs 2.10

Silence the outer through love and the inner becomes more clear.

YOU SHALL NOT TAKE
VENGEANCE OR BEAR A GRUDGE
AGAINST ANY OF YOUR PEOPLE,
BUT YOU SHALL LOVE YOUR
NEIGHBOR AS YOURSELF:

I AM THE LORD.

— Leviticus 19.18

Silence the outer through love and the inner
becomes more clear.

THE ALIEN WHO RESIDES WITH YOU SHALL BE TO YOU AS THE CITIZEN AMONG YOU; YOU SHALL LOVE THE ALIEN AS YOURSELF, FOR YOU WERE ALIENS IN THE LAND OF EGYPT: I AM THE LORD YOUR GOD.

— Leviticus 19.34

Love is all that is all else is the illusion.

YOU SHALL LOVE THE LORD YOUR GOD WITH ALL YOUR HEART, AND WITH ALL YOUR SOUL, AND WITH ALL YOUR MIGHT.

— Deuteronomy 6.5

Love Yourself = Love God.

THEN SHE SAID TO HIM,
'HOW CAN YOU SAY,
I love you
WHEN YOUR HEART
IS NOT WITH ME?
— Judges 16.15
When the heart is open
no words are necessary.

THEN JONATHAN MADE A COVENANT WITH DAVID, BECAUSE HE LOVED HIM AS HIS OWN SOUL.

— 1 Samuel 18.3

We are all apart of the infinite oneness.

'O LORD GOD OF HEAVEN, THE GREAT AND AWESOME GOD WHO KEEPS COVENANT AND STEADFAST LOVE WITH THOSE WHO LOVE HIM AND KEEP HIS COMMANDMENTS;

— Nehemiah 1.5

Steadfast love: unwavering love - unconditioned love — poised love

FOR WE ARE SLAVES; YET OUR GOD HAS NOT FORSAKEN US IN OUR SLAVERY, BUT HAS EXTENDED TO US HIS STEADFAST LOVE BEFORE THE KINGS OF PERSIA, TO GIVE US NEW LIFE TO SET UP THE HOUSE OF OUR GOD,

— Ezra 9.9

Steadfast love: unwavering love-unconditioned love — poised love

YOU HAVE GRANTED ME LIFE AND STEADFAST LOVE, AND YOUR CARE HAS PRESERVED MY SPIRIT.

— Job 10.12

Steadfast love: unwavering love - unconditioned love — poised love

THEREFORE BE IMITATORS OF GOD, AS BELOVED CHILDREN.

— Ephesians 5.1

We are the co-creators of our life.

In the same way, husbands should love their wives as they do their own bodies. He who loves his wife loves himself.

— Ephesians 5.28

Mirrors, reflecting to us more disowned parts to love.

Grace be with all who have an undying love for our Lord Jesus Christ

— Ephesians 6.24

Grace is not just peace and support. Grace is a state only experienced when both peace and war, support and challenge are observed and appreciated equally as equals for what they are, as they are, and then and only then can the heart open to a true state of Grace, Gratis, Gracias, Gratitude.

And this is my prayer, that
your love may overflow more
and more
with knowledge
and full insight

— Philippians 1.9

In the center.

I want their hearts to be encouraged and united in love, so that they may have all the riches of assured understanding and have the knowledge of God's mystery,

— Colossians 2.2

Centered, poised and equilibrated

i love you

And indeed you do love all the brothers and sisters throughout Macedonia. But we urge you, beloved, to do so more and more,

— 1 Thessalonians 4.10

We all have an infinite amount of the universe to love.

May the Lord
direct your hearts
to the love of God
and to the
steadfastness of
Christ.

— 2 Thessalonians 3.5

Love

THEREFORE, MY DEAR FRIENDS, FLEE FROM THE WORSHIP OF IDOLS.

— 1 Corinthians 10.14

Look to the inner, all else is an idol.

Love never ends. But as for prophecies, they will come to an end; as for tongues, they will cease; as for knowledge, it will come to an end.

— 1 Corinthians 13.8

Love is all there is all else is illusion.

PURSUE LOVE AND STRIVE FOR THE SPIRITUAL GIFTS, AND ESPECIALLY THAT YOU MAY PROPHESY.

— 1 CORINTHIANS 14.1

In the center of equilibrium resides all that is, all that was and all that will be. Get there and you will see glimpses of your destiny.

Let all that you do be done in love.

— 1 CORINTHIANS 16.14

Love is all there is all else is illusion.

For the whole law is summed
up in a single commandment,
'You shall love your neighbor as
yourself.'

— GALATIANS 5.14

Mirrors give us the power to love more.

Just as he
chose us
in Christ
before the
foundation of
the world to be
holy and blameless
before him in love.

— Ephesians 1.4

Find the center you may see something that
amazes you.

And that Christ may dwell in your hearts through faith, as you are being rooted and grounded in love.

— Ephesians 3.17

Love is inside all of us so deeply rooted we can only see and feel the surface.

ALL MY INTIMATE FRIENDS ABHOR ME, AND THOSE WHOM I LOVED HAVE TURNED AGAINST ME.

— Job 19.19

In order for a tree to grow it must shed branches.

BUT I, THROUGH THE ABUNDANCE OF YOUR STEADFAST LOVE, WILL ENTER YOUR HOUSE. I WILL BOW DOWN TOWARDS YOUR HOLY TEMPLE IN AWE OF YOU.

— Psalms 5.7

Only through our unconditional love can we enter.

For your steadfast love is before my eyes, and I walk in faithfulness to you.

— Psalms 26.3:

Open your heart through balance and see the unconditional love.

O LORD, I LOVE THE HOUSE IN WHICH YOU DWELL, AND THE PLACE WHERE YOUR GLORY ABIDES.

— PSALMS 26.8

At the center, in balance is where this exists.

Let your face shine upon your servant; save me in your steadfast love.

— PSALMS 31.16

Open your heart, you will experience this.

MANY ARE THE TORMENTS OF THE WICKED, BUT STEADFAST LOVE SURROUNDS THOSE WHO TRUST IN THE LORD

— Psalms 32.10

Love is all around us 24 his 7 days a week 365 days a year. All we have to do is open our eyes to equilibrium and we will see that love.

O continue your steadfast love to those who know you, and your salvation to the upright of heart!

— Psalms 36.10

Love is in the heart, open it and you will see it.

the children of his
servants shall inherit
it, and those who love
his name shall live in it.

— PSALMS 69.36

The center, love, it is available to us all.

Great peace have those who love your law; nothing can make them stumble.

— PSALMS 119.165

The law is equilibrium.

A SCOFFER WHO IS REBUKED WILL ONLY HATE YOU; THE WISE, WHEN REBUKED, WILL LOVE YOU.

— PROVERBS 9.8

All the world is our mirror, to love more.

WHOEVER LOVES DISCIPLINE LOVES KNOWLEDGE.

— PROVERBS 12.1

Discipline: from Latin disciplina:
teaching, learning

TO GET WISDOM IS TO LOVE ONESELF;

— PROVERBS 19.8

Nothing could be more true.

FOR YOU LOVE ALL THINGS
THAT EXIST,
AND DETEST
NONE OF THE
THINGS THAT
YOU HAVE MADE,
FOR YOU WOULD NOT
HAVE MADE ANYTHING IF YOU
HAD HATED IT.

— Wisdom of Solomon 11.24

Everything serves.

IN YOUR STEADFAST LOVE YOU LED THE PEOPLE WHOM YOU REDEEMED; YOU GUIDED THEM BY YOUR STRENGTH TO YOUR HOLY ABODE.

— EXODUS 15.13

Seeing the balance in what we see gets us to this holy abode.

NO

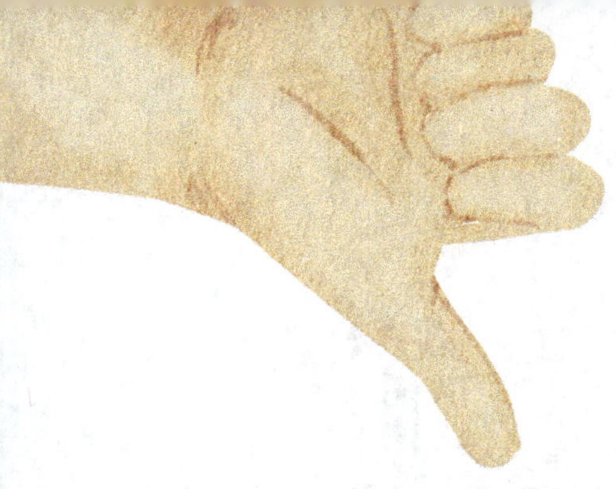

Thou shalt not covet thy neighbor's house, thou shalt not covet thy neighbor's wife, nor his manservant, nor his maidservant, nor his ox, nor his ass, nor any thing that is thy neighbor's.

— **Exodus 17**

Everything is present. We may not see the form in which we have it in our lives, but it is there.

No one can serve two masters; for a slave will either hate the one and love the other, or be devoted to the one and despise the other. You cannot serve God and Wealth.

— Matthew 6.24

Live the why that you where put here to do, and become wealthy while doing it and you serve only one, God. Because he put you here to do something only you can do. In other words follow your inspirations not your desperations.

HONOR YOUR FATHER AND MOTHER; ALSO, YOU SHALL LOVE YOUR NEIGHBOR AS YOURSELF."

— Matthew 19.19

Let the reflections allow us to love more of ourselves.

AND A SECOND IS LIKE IT:

"YOU SHALL LOVE YOUR NEIGHBOR AS YOURSELF."

— Matthew 22.39

Love is all that is, all else is illusion.

YOU SHALL LOVE THE LORD YOUR GOD WITH ALL YOUR HEART, AND WITH ALL YOUR SOUL, AND WITH ALL YOUR MIND, AND WITH ALL YOUR STRENGTH.

— Mark 12.30

See the magnificent balance in life and you will love God with all that you are.

THE SECOND IS THIS, "YOU SHALL LOVE YOUR NEIGHBOR AS YOURSELF." THERE IS NO OTHER COMMANDMENT GREATER THAN THESE.'

— Mark 12.31

Life is our mirror, to teach us love.

THE FATHER LOVES THE SON AND HAS PLACED ALL THINGS IN HIS HANDS.

— John 3.35

All of creation is present in frequencies we can tune into or tune out of any time we'd love to.

The Father loves the Son and shows him all that he himself is doing; and he will show him greater works than these, so that you will be astonished.

— John 5.20

Love life and yourself for what it is as it is and so will be revealed.

If you keep my
commandments, you will abide
in my love, just as I have kept
my Father's commandments
and abide in his love.

— John 15.10

Equilibrium and balance leads to this love.

Good
Evil

LET LOVE BE GENUINE; HATE WHAT IS EVIL, HOLD FAST TO WHAT IS GOOD;

— ROMANS 12.9

Everything in life has both sides.

Owe no one anything, except to love one another, for the one who loves another has fulfilled the law.

— **Romans 13.8**

Wow, Gods law is love.

BUT, AS IT IS WRITTEN, WHAT NO EYE HAS SEEN, NOR EAR HEARD, NOR THE HUMAN HEART CONCEIVED, WHAT GOD HAS PREPARED FOR THOSE WHO LOVE HIM"=

— 1 Corinthians 2.9

In the center of equilibrium resides all that is, all that was and all that will be.

NOW CONCERNING FOOD SACRIFICED TO IDOLS: WE KNOW THAT 'ALL OF US POSSESS KNOWLEDGE.' KNOWLEDGE PUFFS UP, BUT LOVE BUILDS UP.

— 1 CORINTHIANS 8.1

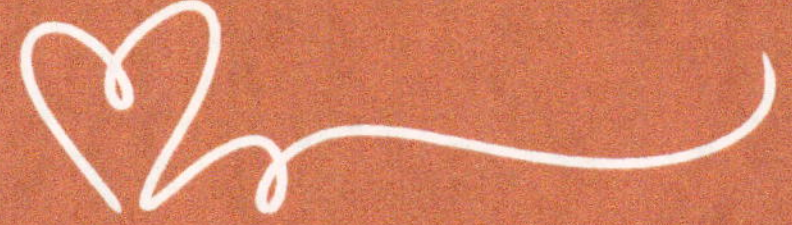

Ego is proud, love is humble.

The Gifts of Wisdom

Does not wisdom call,
and does not understanding raise her voice? On
the heights, beside the way,
at the crossroads she takes her stand; beside the
gates in front of the town,
at the entrance of the portals she cries out: `To
you, O people, I call,
and my cry is to all that live.
O simple ones, learn prudence;
acquire intelligence, you who lack it. Hear, for I
will speak noble things,
and from my lips will come what is right; for my
mouth will utter truth;
wickedness is an abomination to my lips.
All the words of my mouth are righteous; there is
nothing twisted or crooked in them.
They are all straight to one who understands
and right to those who find knowledge.
Take my instruction instead of silver,
and knowledge rather than choice gold; for
wisdom is better than jewels,
and all that you may desire cannot compare with
her.

The Gifts of Wisdom
2 of 2

and all that you may desire cannot compare with
her.
I, wisdom, live with prudence,
and I attain knowledge and discretion. The fear
of the Lord is hatred of evil. Pride and arrogance
and the way of evil and perverted speech I hate.
I have good advice and sound wisdom; I have
insight, I have strength.
By me kings reign,
and rulers decree what is just;
by me rulers rule,
and nobles, all who govern rightly. I love those
who love me,
and those who seek me diligently find me. Riches
and honor are with me,
enduring wealth and prosperity.
My fruit is better than gold, even fine gold, and
my yield than choice silver.
I walk in the way of righteousness, along the
paths of justice,
endowing with wealth those who love me, and
filling their treasuries.

— Proverb 8

Wisdom Part in Creation
1 of 2

The Lord created me at the beginning of his work,
the first of his acts of long ago.
Ages ago I was set up,
at the first, before the beginning of the earth.
When there were no depths I was brought forth,
when there were no springs abounding with
water. Before the mountains had been shaped,
before the hills, I was brought forth—
when he had not yet made earth and fields,
or the world's first bits of soil.
When he established the heavens, I was there,
when he drew a circle on the face of the deep,
when he made firm the skies above,
when he established the fountains of the deep,
when he assigned to the sea its limit,
so that the waters might not transgress his
command, when he marked out the foundations
of the earth,
then I was beside him, like a master worker;

Wisdom Part in Creation

and I was daily his delight,
rejoicing before him always, rejoicing in his
inhabited world and delighting in the human
race.
'And now, my children, listen to me:
happy are those who keep my ways.
Hear instruction and be wise, and do not neglect
it.
Happy is the one who listens to me,
watching daily at my gates,
waiting beside my doors.
For whoever finds me finds life
and obtains favor from the Lord;
but those who miss me injure themselves;
all who hate me love death.'

When we are centered, poised and equilibrated.

GOD'S LOVE,

light and wisdom are surrounding us every moment of everyday. It is up to us to see them. They intertwine in our lives in a magnificent dance of equilibrium. Both supporting us and challenging us simultaneously, sitting waiting for us to see the beautiful dance of life that is Love.

All my love
Gary Steele